About the Consumer Financial Protection Bureau

The Consumer Financial Protection Bureau, or the CFPB, is focused on making markets for consumer financial products and services work for Americans–whether they are applying for a mortgage, choosing among credit cards, or using any number of other consumer financial products. We empower consumers to take more control over their financial lives.

The CFPB Office for Older Americans is the only federal office dedicated to the financial health of Americans age 62 and over. Along with other agencies, the Office works to support sound financial decision-making by consumers to help them reach their own life goals, and to prevent financial exploitation of older adults.

For more information about the CFPB, see consumerfinance.gov.

About this guide

To help assisted living and nursing facility managers and staff prevent and address elder financial exploitation of their residents, the Office for Older Americans contracted and worked closely with Iris Freeman, MSW, William Mitchell College of Law, to prepare this guide. The guide is not intended to provide legal advice or serve as a substitute for your own legal counsel. If you have questions or concerns about legal issues and responsibilities, we recommend that you seek the guidance of the appropriate legal professional.

What's inside

Introduction

Mr. R, age 77, suffered from Alzheimer's and Parkinson's diseases, diabetes and other ailments. His pastor persuaded the former church deacon to grant him authority to manage his finances and care decisions. The result of this misplaced trust included 130 ATM withdrawals from Mr. R's bank account, nine months of unpaid nursing home bills, and the threat of discharge for nonpayment. The victim died at his facility. The perpetrator was charged and convicted of financial exploitation of a vulnerable adult.

When an older person in an assisted living or nursing facility is the target of financial abuse, everyone suffers. Financial losses affect the resident, the facility, and the broader community. The primary victim is the vulnerable resident, robbed of economic security and placed at risk of involuntary discharge or loss of housing for nonpayment.

Sadly, the people exploiting older adults are often family members or other trusted people who are handling the financial affairs of an incapacitated parent, relative or friend. The financial arrangement may be informal—or based on a formal grant of authority to a fiduciary (such as an agent under power of attorney or a guardian). The financial wrongdoing may have begun at the time of admission or may go back months or years. Intervention, however, rarely begins until the exploitation causes repeated non-payment and staggering over-due bills. While most family members or others in positions of trust are worthy of the confidence we place in them, you as a facility operator or staff member should act, promptly, when people violate that trust.

As a care provider, you are in a unique position to help protect older residents from exploitation. You can prevent abuse or intervene early when the threat is from:

- trusted persons handling financial affairs

- stranger scams, and

- theft by staff or intruders.

Your key role in the daily lives of residents enables you to stand guard and jump in when your resident is in jeopardy. This guide will help you be ready.

This manual focuses primarily on exploitation by trusted persons but also includes material about responding to scams and other types of theft.

Purpose and scope

This guide aims to help operators and staff of nursing facilities and assisted living residences protect the people in their care from financial exploitation through prevention and early intervention. The manual is for administrators as well as business office staff, social service personnel and any staff members involved in the admissions process. Much of the information about warning signs and building awareness among staff and residents may be useful in other residential settings for older people or for people with disabilities.

We outline ways to create awareness, policies and processes to protect the facility residents. State laws vary, so you should also become familiar with your state's laws, regulations, mandates, reporting requirements and systems. We encourage you and colleagues in your state to add your state-specific requirements and processes to this manual. You can create your own state-specific manual by adding content about state laws, practices and resources.[1]

Four pillars of successful intervention

This manual will walk you through four key actions for protecting your residents from financial abuse:

- Prevent – through awareness and training

- Recognize – spot the warning signs and take action

- Record – document your findings, and

- Report – tell the appropriate authorities and trigger responses.

Stay tuned for the **model response protocol** on page 16.

What is elder financial exploitation?

A Prescott, Arizona resident was arrested for stealing over $100,000 from a 74-year-old woman with dementia. The charges included felony theft, fraud, and misuse of a power of attorney. Police were alerted after the victim was approximately $20,000 behind in payments to her care facility. The investigation revealed that the alleged perpetrator sold the victim's home to a relative for less than fair market value and took control of various other assets.

Family, friends, neighbors, caregivers, fiduciaries, business people, and others may try to take advantage of an older person. They may take money without permission, fail to repay money they owe, charge too much for services, or just not do what they were paid to do. These are examples of financial exploitation or financial abuse.[2] Financial exploitation is a form of elder abuse.

The crime of the 21st century

Here are some numbers that show the seriousness of the threat:

Losses are huge: one study estimated that older Americans lost at least $2.9 billion to financial exploitation by a broad spectrum of perpetrators in 2010, although many experts believe the true cost is much higher.

Financial exploitation is the most common form of elder abuse—a recent study concluded that about five percent of Americans 60+ experienced financial mistreatment by a family member in a single year.

This epidemic is truly under the radar: a 2011 study found that protective services agencies or programs for victims reached only one in 44 cases of financial exploitation.

Most exploitation complaints to long-term care ombudsmen involve perpetrators from outside the facility.

While everyone, regardless of age, is a potential victim of theft and other financial crimes, older Americans are at greater risk than the general population. Cognitive impairment diminishes the ability of older adults to make financial decisions and to detect frauds and scams. Many older people have cognitive impairments: an estimated 22% percent of Americans over age seventy have mild cognitive impairment, and one in eight Americans aged 65+ has Alzheimer's disease. The percentage of congregate care residents with cognitive impairment is much higher than the general older population: about half of nursing facility residents—and over 40% of residents in assisted living and board and care homes—have dementia. Finally, new brain research suggests that the risk of financial exploitation in later life may occur even when older people do not have mild cognitive impairment or dementia.

As family and other trusted persons step in or are brought in to manage an elder's finances, some elders succumb to victimization, leaving them destitute and their care facilities unpaid.

Financial exploitation takes many different forms. Someone with a legal obligation to handle the vulnerable person's finances may fail to use the funds for necessities like food, clothing, shelter and health care, putting the vulnerable adult at risk of harm. People with legal obligations to handle finances include fiduciaries such as agents under power of attorney, trustees, guardians, Social Security representative payees and VA fiduciaries.

In other cases, the perpetrator may have no legal obligation to take care of a vulnerable person's money. Someone may take possession of and control the vulnerable resident's property by pressuring, misleading or lying to the vulnerable person, or gain the vulnerable adult's trust by professing to love and promising to care for him/her if they can just share a bank account.

Elder financial exploitation cases are complex. Financial exploitation often occurs in relationships where the vulnerable person has placed his/her trust and confidence in another person. (Confidence, in this sense, is the origin of the phrase, "con game.") When family members are perpetrators, the subtleties of family history, sibling conflicts, and expectations concerning

Definitions

Elder abuse, often referred to as "abuse, neglect and exploitation," includes many types of mistreatment of older adults. The National Center on Elder Abuse describes seven types of elder abuse:

- Physical Abuse

- Sexual Abuse

- Emotional or Psychological Abuse

- Neglect

- Abandonment

- Financial or Material Exploitation

- Self-neglect.

Terminology for these types of elder abuse varies in state law.

Vulnerable adult, person, or resident—an individual who is at risk of abuse, neglect or exploitation because of age or disability.

estate management and inheritance may surface. Financial abuse may be accompanied by other types of mistreatment, such as emotional abuse or neglect of care.

For the victim, the losses are more extensive than dollars and property. Financial exploitation can cause severe emotional distress, depression, deterioration of physical health, loss of independence, and a shortened lifespan. Despite the exploitation, the victim may continue to feel dependent on and protective of the perpetrator.

Understanding the laws

When Mrs. B was 72 she sold her mobile home and moved in with her daughter and granddaughter in Monterey, Calif. She decided she didn't want to deal with her finances any longer and let the two take control. But her daughter and granddaughter drained Mrs. B of jewelry, furniture, and an annuity worth almost $90,000, and abandoned her at a nursing facility, according to court documents. They were convicted of grand theft and financial elder abuse, both felonies.

State Laws and Response Systems

Your state's laws include definitions of financial exploitation, reporting mandates (if any), criminal sanctions and other important guidance. The primary agencies that investigate reports of suspected elder financial exploitation are Adult Protective Services (APS), licensing agencies, law enforcement, and the long-term care ombudsman. Nearly all states require health care providers to report suspected abuse, neglect and exploitation (referred to as mandatory reporters in this guide) to APS or another public authority. APS, however, does not carry out facility investigations in every state, so you should know which agency is responsible for investigating financial exploitation of residents in your care setting.

Adult Protective Services

Frequently, APS workers are the first to respond in cases of abuse, neglect or exploitation. APS workers evaluate two things before opening an investigation:

- whether the alleged victim is *eligible* for protective services, and

- whether the information reported *meets the legal definition* of abuse, neglect or exploitation in their state or locality.

Eligibility for protective services. Your state's law specifies whether the alleged victim meets the definition of an adult eligible for protective services. In some states, for example, APS will investigate alleged abuse of adults aged 18 or older who are vulnerable due to a physical or mental impairment. In other states, APS investigates abuse allegations when the alleged victim is over a certain age, e.g. 60 or 65, regardless of disability. However, most states have both criteria: an age criterion as well as a condition criterion (e.g. physical or mental impairment, dementia, etc.).

Definition of mistreatment. Similarly, APS workers look at whether the allegations in a given case meet the state's definition of financial exploitation. You should know how your state defines elder financial exploitation. Your APS agency can provide this information. This definition helps you to know what to watch out for and what facts to include when reporting suspected abuse to a local or state agency.

If APS finds that the person has experienced or is at risk of experiencing financial exploitation, APS decides what services, if any, are necessary for the vulnerable adult's safety or well-being and recommends a service plan.

While everyone in every state should report suspected financial exploitation to APS, almost all states have some form of mandatory reporting of elder financial exploitation. Some states require reporting by specific categories of professionals and providers. Other states require "any person" to report. It is important to review your state laws to learn whether you—and members of your staff—have a mandatory obligation to report.[4] Talk to your facility lawyer or corporate compliance department to get updated information about reporting requirements. Even if reporting is not mandated, any concerned person may and should voluntarily make a report when he or she suspects financial exploitation.

Individuals who are offered APS services have the legal right to decline help (if they have decision-making capacity). The victim has a right to refuse services even when a mandated reporter, service provider, advocate, and the APS investigator believe services may be appropriate. Talk to APS personnel in your state about how they determine whether a victim has the capacity to decline help.

Law Enforcement

Reporting suspected exploitation to law enforcement also is

Definitions

Adult protective services (APS) are social services programs provided by states nationwide, serving seniors and adults with disabilities who are in need of assistance. Adult protective services is a generic term, not necessarily the name of the agency in your state.[3] APS workers frequently serve as first responders in cases of abuse, neglect or exploitation. The National Adult Protective Services Association website provides information about how to report suspected abuse in each state. www. napsa-now.org/get-help/ help-in-your-area.

Long-term Care Ombudsmen are advocates for residents of nursing facilities, board and care homes, assisted living facilities and similar adult care facilities, in programs administered by the federal Administration on Aging/Administration for Community Living. Ombudsman staff and volunteers work to resolve problems and concerns of individual residents. Every state has an Office of the State Long-Term Care Ombudsman, headed by a full-time state ombudsman.

critically important. In some states, reporting to law enforcement is mandatory. Financial exploitation may violate an array of criminal laws. Some states have enacted laws making elder financial exploitation a specific crime. But generally law enforcement personnel investigate and prosecutors charge people with other crimes such as theft, larceny, embezzlement, forgery, fraud and money laundering.

Your facility or company lawyers or compliance officers should be able to provide details about your state's criminal code provisions. Local law enforcement agencies and local prosecutors also may be able to help. Communicating and coordinating with law enforcement will help ensure that you report suspected criminal acts. You can also get help with training your staff and enhance working relationships.

Federal Reporting Requirements

In addition to state mandatory reporting laws, federal law[5] requires long-term care facilities[6] that receive at least $10,000 in federal funds during the preceding year to report suspected crimes against a resident to state survey agencies and to local law enforcement.

Specifically, the law requires that the owner, operator, employee, manager, agent, or contractor of a covered facility report "any reasonable suspicion of a crime," as defined by local law, committed against a resident of, or someone receiving care from, the facility. If the victim has serious bodily injury, covered individuals must report immediately upon suspicion, but no later than two hours after the suspicion occurs. Other reports must be made no later than 24 hours after forming the suspicion.

Covered individuals are subject to penalties for failure to fulfill these obligations. Facilities must notify covered individuals (e.g. employees and contractors) of their duties annually. In addition, facilities must post conspicuous notice of employees' rights, including protections from retaliation for carrying out their responsibilities under this law.[7]

Definitions

Mandatory reporters are people required by law to report their suspicions about elder abuse to a specified public authority.

Warning signs that *may* indicate financial exploitation

Mr. C was charged with stealing more than $315,000 from his elderly mother's retirement accounts over the course of five years. According to the criminal complaint, he was named as his mother's agent under a power of attorney. Prudent investment and funds from long-term care insurance should have been sufficient to cover his mother's care for the rest of her life, yet she was evicted from her assisted living residence for nonpayment. In the process of searching for a less expensive facility, another of the victim's children uncovered the theft. Over the years, the vast majority of withdrawals had been made at a casino.

A variety of things you observe or detect may signal that a resident is a victim of financial exploitation. Here is a list of many of the "red flags" that you might spot.

Things a resident tells you or that you observe concerning the resident

- Resident, regardless of cognitive impairment, complains or reports that someone is misusing or stealing his/her money or property

- Resident reports missing checkbook, credit card, or important papers

- Resident is agitated or distraught prior to or after a family member or friend visits

- Resident is agitated or distraught prior to or after a family member or friend takes him/her out for a visit or appointment

- Resident becomes secretive and suddenly starts hiding possessions or hoarding papers

Things you observe in or about a resident's room or apartment

- Disappearance of possessions

- Replacement of possessions in resident's room with those of lesser value

- Resident lacks basics (e.g. underwear) but personal needs account is depleted

- Blank deposit slips or withdrawal forms in conspicuous places for easy taking

- Missing or unaccounted for medications

Family dynamics and other observations when the resident is with visitors

- Observing/hearing a resident pressured to make a decision or sign a document "now"

- Observing/hearing a resident being threatened by family or other visitor that unless the resident agrees to or signs a document, the visitor will stop taking care of the resident

- "Chaperoning" - suspected person lets others visit only when he/she is present and insists on speaking for the resident

- New acquaintance showing intense affection for resident, isolating her/him from others

- Previously uninvolved persons claim authority to manage resident's care and/or finances but do not provide documentation

- Agent or family member declines or pressures resident to decline prescribed treatment(s) on the basis of cost, overriding the resident's wishes

- Family members or fiduciaries avoiding care plan meetings or failing to return calls from facility staff

- Known gambling, drug or alcohol problem of resident, family member or visitor

- Conflicts concerning finances between resident's adult children or others with close relationships to the resident

Billing issues

- Unpaid facility bills

- Unpaid pharmacy bills

- Stalling or broken promises from person handling resident's money

- Abrupt or repeated changes in responsibility for paying resident's bills

- Bills paid in cash

- Communication from a family member, friend, fiduciary or partner that he or she plans to move the resident after questions arise about suspected financial exploitation

Power of Attorney Matters

- Agent under power of attorney failing to provide necessary documentation

- Multiple agents under powers of attorney in conflict over responsibility to pay the facility bill

- Resident who appears to lack decision-making capacity signs new power of attorney document

Checks and Imbalances

- Checks or other documents signed/dated when resident is no longer able to write

- Suspicious signatures (e.g. many versions of a resident's signature or one that was shaky is suddenly firm or *vice versa*)

- Resident's checkbook or check register shows checks made out to "cash" frequently and/or check numbers out of sequence

- Telephone card or telephone bill fees for calls not made by the resident or otherwise unauthorized by the resident (called "cramming")

- Credit card charges for items not purchased by the resident

- Erratic use of personal needs allowance by family member or fiduciary

- Gifts (either frequent or costly) to staff or volunteers

- Sales of valuables to facility staff or volunteers.

Model response protocol: recognize, record & report

Mrs. A, who suffered a series of strokes, had named her daughter as agent under a power of attorney to pay her nursing home bills. Instead, her daughter, Lisa, wrote checks to herself and to pay for her own groceries and personal items. The daughter then moved her mother from one skilled nursing facility to another because of arrearages. An ombudsman, who became involved during the victim's second placement, noted that the second home similarly discharged the resident and wrote off the bills. At the third nursing home, the ombudsman, adult protective services and the police directly addressed the financial exploitation of the resident and arranged stable housing for her. Prosecutors charged the daughter, and she pleaded guilty to one count of theft by swindle for taking $22,000.

Establish and maintain a team approach to financial security.

Prevention of financial exploitation is the number one goal, and awareness and training are keys to prevention. However, your other top priorities should be early recognition, documentation and reporting. In fact, these activities also contribute to prevention—since financial abuse is often ongoing, early identification of a problem can help "stop the bleeding."

Assemble a team that will form your facility's frontline on financial exploitation. The team should include at least the administrator, business office representative, and social work representative as team members. The team should implement a system for early, effective responses to perceived financial exploitation through regular periodic meetings, case review, and coordinated action. Consider adding other staff, such as your Admissions Coordinator, to the group. The system should be part of any corporate compliance plan.

Establish which member has the lead responsibility for record-keeping and reporting cases of suspected financial exploitation. In nursing facilities, the compliance officer would most likely have that role. The administrator should designate a back-up person in case the lead person is unavailable.

Provide training for the team on your objectives for preventing and responding to financial exploitation, the jurisdictions and boundaries of pertinent agencies, as well as the interactions among these agencies.

Without a solid team approach, led by the administrator, hectic days in a facility and periodic changes in staffing can allow a bad situation to endure and exploitation to continue. An effective team promotes the safety of the resident and the financial security of the facility.

Investigate and record as soon as warning signs appear

- When suspicions arise, call a meeting of the team. The trigger might be an account that is delinquent for sixty days—or any of the red flags listed above.

- Consult with other staff members who may have observed relevant behavior and be sure that they document each instance of that behavior with the date, time, what was observed, and the names of and contact information for witness(es).

- Direct care and housekeeping or maintenance staff may be the most familiar with the resident. Encourage them to talk with you about their concerns and include their observations in the record.

- Document all pertinent communications such as phone calls, meetings, and letters. Investigators will need dates, times, locations, behaviors/statements, physical evidence, and the names of witnesses.

Advocate for the vulnerable resident

- Talk with the resident separately from the individual(s) suspected of exploitation. Note inconsistencies in their stories. Ask open-ended questions. Take note of nonverbal cues in your conversation, as well as those you observe when the resident and suspected exploiter(s) are together. The resident may be hesitant to acknowledge a loved one's financial missteps due to guilt, fear of retaliation, or sympathy for the exploitative person, particularly when the resident has rescued the person from trouble repeatedly. However, with support from a trusted advocate, a victim who refuses to acknowledge abuse or exploitation may later develop the courage to talk about the experience.

- The social worker or other designated staff member should inform the resident about the regional or local Long-term Care Ombudsman Program and assist the resident with contacting that office. If there is an ombudsman visitor who comes to the facility periodically, the resident may prefer talking to that individual instead of making a call for help. Facility staff should not contact the ombudsman solely because the resident is at risk of discharge for nonpayment.

  - The ombudsman's role is to respond directly to the resident and to act on behalf of residents, not providers. If you reach out to the ombudsman for assistance when a resident is cognitively or physically unable to make the request, you should document the resident's incapacity to contact the ombudsman and the actions you have taken to protect the resident from exploitation.

  - When a resident cannot consent and does not have a legally authorized surrogate—or the local ombudsman determines that a legal representative is not acting in the resident's best interest—the local ombudsman takes guidance from the state ombudsman director on how to proceed. The state ombudsman uses an established protocol to take action on behalf of a resident who cannot make or communicate decisions.

Understand reporting requirements

- Be aware of your state's laws about reporting suspected financial exploitation. Learn the following things about your state's laws:

  - whether you—and members of your staff—are mandatory reporters to APS or another public authority

  - whether you have additional reporting obligations to law enforcement and/or licensing agencies

  - who is eligible for protective services

  - which agency investigates financial exploitation in your type of facility.

- Understand the immunity provisions in your state's laws—and reassure your staff that there are "safe harbors" for reporting suspected abuse. Almost all states have provisions providing immunity for good faith reporting of suspected elder financial exploitation. This means that you can't be held liable if it turns out that the activity you observed wasn't exploitation, as long as you made the report in good faith (or a similar standard spelled out in your laws). In most states, this immunity extends to civil, criminal, or administrative actions. Generally this immunity also applies to other activities that may stem from those reports (such as testifying in a court or administrative proceeding).

- Remember that federal law requires nursing home providers and specific "covered individuals" to report suspected crimes against a resident to local law enforcement. Understanding how your state defines crimes involving financial exploitation will help you fulfill this reporting obligation.

- Document your information as thoroughly as you can, but remember that you are reporting a reasonable suspicion, not investigating a crime or proving a case. Think of the reporter's role as that of a traditional newspaper reporter. Keep notes to the degree possible on who, what, where, when, and how.

Make a report: who, what, where, when and how

- Report financial exploitation of a vulnerable resident in accordance with state and federal law.

- When you report suspected elder financial exploitation to local authorities, state that you are requesting an investigation of financial exploitation of a vulnerable resident or whatever terminology your state uses.

- Your allegation should include facts that support and illustrate the report. Your state's law may list the things you should include in your report. Here are some basic components of a complete report to authorities of any kind:

  - the time and date of the report

  - the name, address, email address and telephone number of the person reporting

  - the time, date, and location of the incident(s)

  - the name(s) of the persons involved, including but not limited to the alleged victim, alleged perpetrator(s) and witness(es)

  - whether you believe there is a risk of imminent danger to the alleged victim

  - a description of the suspected financial exploitation and signs of any other type of abuse or neglect

  - the alleged victim's disability and/or health condition including any information on cognitive status

- the relationship of the alleged perpetrator to the alleged victim, if known

- whether a report has been made to any other public agency, and

- whether the facility has conducted an internal investigation and the contact information for the individual(s) responsible for the investigation.

- While there are specific federal requirements for nursing homes to report financial crimes directly to law enforcement, staff in any facility should report suspected exploitation, theft and any other financial crime directly to local law enforcement, just as you would in your own home.

Fact or fiction?

Sometimes staff at a protective services, law enforcement or licensing agency will claim that a discharge notice is required before you may make a report. **This is not true.** Regardless of whether a resident has a delinquent account or is facing discharge from the facility, the agency should accept a report and assign the case for investigation.

Follow-up makes a difference

If you are unsatisfied with a public agency's response to your report, you may be able to make headway with additional information. Ask directly whether additional information would help in the investigation. Ask to discuss the case with a supervisor. Contact your state's provider or professional organization for advice on how to work more effectively with the public agency. You may not have to accept NO as the one and only answer. Be aware, however, that the agency may be bound by confidentiality restrictions that preclude it from sharing the information. APS may not be able to share any information about a case without the client's express permission. It may appear to you and others in the community that APS did not respond, offer or provide services, when in fact the agency did as much as it could.

Document each conversation you have with agency officials for future reference, noting the names of contacts and the dates and times of your conversations.

Unfortunately, national trends indicate an increasing demand for APS services without growth in investigative staff. In response, APS agencies may prioritize case types and may not have the capacity to respond to all reports. The resulting triage of cases inevitably causes frustration for people whose reports do not trigger an investigation. But keep at it when you believe your resident has been victimized and needs help.

Additional avenues for action when you suspect financial abuse of a resident

Contact the local **Social Security** office if you suspect that a representative payee is misusing a resident's Social Security benefits. You may also call the Social Security Administration to report possible misuse at Social Security's toll-free number, 1-800-772-1213, between 7 a.m. and 7 p.m. on business days.

If the resident needs a new payee, make an effort to assist in identifying an alternative family member or trusted person who can offer to serve as representative payee. Representative payee applications are available at the local Social Security office. As a last resort, the provider can be the representative payee, unless prohibited by state law. As a general principle, there is an inherent conflict of interest when one entity has the simultaneous authority to bill for payment and to pay the bills. For more information, consult the Social Security Administration's guide for organizational representative payees. www.ssa.gov/payee/NewGuide/toc.htm.

Contact the **Department of Veterans Affairs** if you suspect financial abuse by a VA fiduciary. The Department provides contact information at https://iris.custhelp.com/app/answers/detail/a_id/3029 or you can use the "contact us" feature at https://iris.custhelp.com/app/ask. For more information about the VA fiduciary program, check www.benefits.va.gov/fiduciary/.

Contact the **court** that appointed the resident's guardian or conservator if you suspect that a guardian or conservator is misusing the resident's funds or property.

Contact the vulnerable resident's **bank, credit union or other financial services provider**. Your notification may trigger an internal investigation and further action by the financial institution, but recognize that without authorization by the owner of the account or a legally authorized fiduciary, you are not entitled to receive any information or follow-up to your "report." Direct your call to a security officer at the bank or financial institution. Also remember that your first call should be to the local authorities who investigate suspected financial exploitation of vulnerable adults in your state and your type of facility.

If the suspected perpetrator is a staff member, contractor or volunteer in the facility

This manual does not include procedures for handling personnel issues when the suspected perpetrator is a staff member. However, be sure to have protocols and processes for responding to suspected cases of exploitation by a staff member, a contractor or a volunteer.

State civil laws

In some states, there are remedies beyond local APS intervention and criminal sanctions. These states have laws to help victims of financial exploitation and their attorneys bring cases in civil court and recover assets. Some states have processes to freeze remaining assets or make it impossible for property transfers to proceed. Learn about the legal options available in your state, and provide general information to victims of financial exploitation and others acting on their behalf. Suggest that victims and those acting on their behalf consult an attorney to explore whether they have civil remedies. Local civil legal services programs (often known as "legal aid") may be able to represent the resident, or the resident may need private counsel.

Getting advice in your community

There will be times when, short of making a formal report, you are looking for information and advice from an ombudsman, adult protective services agency or law enforcement agency. Agency and organizational policies differ on whether these agencies accept and respond to requests for consultation or whether they will accept only formal reports. In addition to their legal counsel, every facility needs someone who is a dependable source for advice and assistance in issues concerning financial exploitation. You should try to identify one useful source in your community or state for advice in handling difficult cases.

Preventing and deterring financial exploitation: orientation, training, and facility policies

"There is a time I was working in a nursing home and one lady was admitted there. I worked with her for several months and she explained to me how her family and investment advisers had colluded and she lost all her money and was now on welfare. She expressed how she missed a lot of things she wanted to do or buy. One thing she really missed was a good deodorant. I took it upon myself to be buying her deodorant and lotion which is liked and missed...I was happy that I added joy and happiness to the life of an old lady who was suffering from depression."

Building awareness through staff orientation and training

Educating staff can help prevent financial exploitation of your residents and encourage compassionate responses. Facility management sets the tone that encourages good faith communication between staff and administration. This guide provides content, such as warning signs, to use as you train your staff. In addition, you can use other resources from the Consumer Financial Protection Bureau, such as *Money Smart for Older Adults* and the *Managing Someone Else's Money* guides. You can find information about those materials on pages 24 and 26.

Invite a police officer or other law enforcement official (particularly one with special knowledge of older victims or financial crimes) and/or an ombudsman to participate in training and answer questions. APS representatives and social service providers also can make good trainers. These are opportunities to open up communication on these difficult topics within the facility as well as between facility staff and local service providers. These events establish a culture in which staff members feel safe in expressing suspicions to facility administrators.

Money Smart for Older Adults

Money Smart for Older Adults (MSOA) is an instructor-led training curriculum developed by the Consumer Financial Protection Bureau (CFPB) and the Federal Deposit Insurance Corporation (FDIC). The program raises awareness among older adults and their caregivers on how to prevent elder financial exploitation and encourages advance planning and informed financial decision-making. The module includes:

- Common types of elder financial exploitation

- Identity theft and medical identity theft

- Scams that target veterans benefits

- Planning for unexpected life events

- How to be financially prepared for disasters.

To download the MSOA module or find upcoming train-the-trainer events, go to www.fdic.gov/moneysmart .

To download the participant/resource guide, go to http://files.consumerfinance.gov/f/201306_cfpb_msoa-participant-guide.pdf and to order hard copies, go to www.promotions.usa.gov/cfpbpubs.html .

Topics for staff orientation and in-service training about financial exploitation

- Provider's commitment to preventing and responding to financial exploitation

- Definitions and warning signs

- Risks of permitting financial exploitation to escalate

- When and how to make reports to Adult Protective Services, licensing agencies and law enforcement

- Overview of financial crimes as defined by your state's laws

- Consequences for perpetrators of financial exploitation under your state's laws

- Provider's policies prohibiting accepting money and loans from residents

- Provider's policies and internal processes for documenting and reporting suspected financial exploitation

- The role of the compliance officer

- Applicable state laws and facility policy for releasing money from personal accounts

- Sales people – how your facility has an "open door" for community involvement while protecting residents from unsuitable or deceptive sales presentations

- Visitors – how your facility balances residents' rights to have visitors with security to protect residents from unlawful intruders

- Financial powers of attorney and health care advance directives

- Role of the Long-Term Care Ombudsman Program

Train everyone on your staff who come in contact with potential victims of elder financial exploitation. This includes nursing staff, social service staff, housekeepers and maintenance workers. Sometimes those without direct care responsibilities may be the first to notice warning signs of trouble.

Sometimes a facility employee suffering from "burnout" or a personal crisis can be more prone to misappropriating resident funds or property. Evaluate your personnel policies and staffing patterns, making changes that reduce stress in the work environment. Develop ways to recognize and respond to staff burnout and personal crisis. Employee assistance programs provide a resource for addressing these challenges. Train managers and provide resources about signs of staff burnout or personal crisis so that they can be alert for risks to residents. Provide clear guidance to prevent behavior that may hurt the employee, the residents in his or her care, and the facility.

Building awareness among residents and their loved ones

Programs for staff should be coupled with programs for residents, family members, and groups such as resident and family councils. For these meetings, too, invite a police officer, ombudsman, APS representative or social service provider to assist with training and answer questions. These sessions can begin an ongoing education process and dialogue.

Topics for resident and family programs about financial exploitation

These sessions should include topics listed above for staff training, with a few additions:

- The person to contact when residents or family members have a concern

- Safeguarding private documents and valuables

- Applicable federal and state laws and facility's policy on releasing money from residents' personal accounts

- Managing someone else's money.

One way to start the conversation is by discussing a financial exploitation case from a newspaper story. The case vignettes in this manual may be a starting point. These opportunities can also encourage a resident or family member to confide concerns about financial exploitation to staff and initiate steps to prevent a situation from worsening.

Help for friends and family managing someone else's money

Millions of Americans are managing money or property for a family member or friend who is unable to pay bills or make financial decisions. This can be very overwhelming. You can provide resources for them as they manage money for your residents.

The CFPB Office for Older Americans released four easy-to-understand booklets to help financial caregivers. The *Managing Someone Else's Money* guides are for fiduciaries—people named to manage money for someone else. There are separate guides for agents under powers of attorney, court-appointed guardians, trustees, and government benefit fiduciaries (Social Security representative payees and VA fiduciaries).

The guides help people acting as fiduciaries in three ways:

- They walk them through their duties.

- They tell them how to watch out for scams and financial exploitation, and what to do if their loved one is a victim.

- They tell them where to go for help.

The guides are available to download on the CFPB website at www. consumerfinance.gov/managing-someone-elses-money.

You can also place free bulk orders at http://promotions.usa.gov/ cfpbpubs.html#special. You could distribute the guides at a family or resident program at your facility.

If your facility has a newsletter, use a resident or family program as an occasion to write an article about preventing financial exploitation. For even wider impact, a resident or family council can sponsor a community forum on preventing, recognizing and reporting financial exploitation at the facility or elsewhere. For example, a "shred-a-thon" event to target identity theft may spur both heightened awareness and local recognition for your resident or family council.

Prevention from day one: facility financial policies and practices

Admission to facility

The time of admission can be confusing and emotional for new residents, families and surrogates. But it's important to provide tools for financial protection of residents at the outset. Give the resident or someone acting on the resident's behalf the following information written in plain language:

- The person on staff who will answer billing or coverage questions and how to reach that individual

- The provider's process for responding to late or missed payments

- In appropriate situations, information on serving as a fiduciary (such as the CFPB's *Managing Someone Else's Money* guides–see page 26)

- Policies and procedures for receiving and handling cash from residents or families

- Facility policies regarding theft of personal property and systems for reporting and responding to allegations

- Recommendations for safeguarding checkbooks and ATM cards, including federal benefit debit cards.

If the resident has a fiduciary, the facility should obtain and keep on file documentation of the fiduciary's authority. Examples include power of attorney instruments, court documents naming a guardian, Social Security representative payee authorization, VA fiduciary appointments and trust documents.

Unless you expect the resident's stay to be short, the resident or resident's representative should file a change of address notice with the Social Security Administration and any other entities that mail benefits.

Recommend that residents safely destroy ATM cards that they are no longer using and that they change the Personal Identification Number (PIN) on a card they intend to use.

Recipients of Social Security and other federal benefits are now required to receive their benefits electronically, either by direct deposit to a bank or credit union account or to a Direct Express Debit MasterCard card account, with certain exceptions. For information on electronic payments and how to protect people in your care, see the Department of the Treasury and the Social Security Administration websites.[8]

Monitoring residents' payments to the facility for room and board and other services

Monitoring payments to the facility is critical, because unpaid bills may be a result of financial exploitation of the resident. Early detection and intervention are keys to preventing the worst-case scenarios of drained resources and imminent discharge. Sometimes non-payment has another cause, such as confusion, inaction on an application for public benefits, or a glitch in a third-party payment. Stay on top of all cases where payment is behind, so residents' needs are met whatever the cause.

A few weeks after move in, review the information discussed at admission with the resident or the resident's fiduciary (when the resident cannot engage in meaningful conversation about financial matters). Answer questions, and identify any problems to address.

Maintain and update documents to track resident payments in the business office. Delinquent account tracking documents will be important support for reports of financial abuse to APS and law enforcement.

Establish a process for examining all accounts that are delinquent for sixty days/two payment cycles. Be alert for warning signs of exploitation, but intervene even if you don't spot those red flags.

Monitoring residents' funds

Establish and follow policies for releasing funds from residents' personal needs (trust) accounts. Policies should clarify when it is appropriate to release funds to someone other than the resident.

Perform periodic quality control reviews on a sample of withdrawals from personal funds or personal needs allowance accounts maintained by the facility.

Be alert to depleted accounts of residents who are without basic necessities, such as undergarments, or who say they cannot participate in special facility outings, such as baseball games, because they cannot afford a ticket or fee.

Exploitation or confusion?

Unpaid bills may be a result of financial exploitation. However, they also may be a sign that families are caught in a maze of rules and paperwork.

You can help minimize confusion—and avoid overdue payments—by working with these family members and other nonprofessionals who are assisting the resident. People who are confused or uncertain may be more likely to work with you than those who may be misappropriating a resident's funds.

Provide support and encouragement at admission and follow-up to people who seem to be overwhelmed and bewildered by their situation or their fiduciary duties. Family members and other authorized representatives often have little knowledge about programs that affect the resident's financial well-being, including Medicare, its limitations, the Medicaid program, and the Medicaid application process. Also, they may not understand their duties when managing someone else's money and may benefit from reading the CFPB's guides (see page 26).

For resources to share with residents and those who assist them, see page 36.

Resident gifts to staff or volunteers

Have and communicate policies that prohibit gifts from residents to staff, with exceptions for small tokens of gratitude or holiday gifts.

Have systems to monitor such transactions and assure compliance. Explain these monitoring procedures to staff and volunteers.

Sales calls and presentations to residents

Establish and follow policies that provide a welcoming "open door" to the community, but be alert for salespeople who pose threats to residents.

Prohibit—or develop vigilant screening processes for—sales events at the facility, including those described by the outside entity as informational. Any time you see a retirement or senior seminar advertised as "educational" or as a "workshop," beware. The true goal may be to sell investment, insurance, or financial products at the seminar or in follow-up calls. (The Consumer Financial Protection Bureau's consumer brochure, *Know your financial adviser,* may be helpful to residents and is available to download at http://files.consumerfinance.gov/f/201311_cfpb_flyer_senior-financial-advisors.pdf.)

Suggest that residents and families share their concerns with you about telephone calls or visits from salespeople. Encourage them to say NO whenever they feel pressured to make a decision or a purchase.

Hiring policies

Criminal background checks are one tool for determining whether an applicant for a staff or volunteer position may pose a risk of financial exploitation. When orienting and training new employees, communicate your expectations and policies on abuse prevention and that each resident's person and property will be protected in your facility.

Responding as a community

Addressing elder financial exploitation would be considerably more straightforward if each community, county and state shared universal protocols and resources. The reality is that procedures and sources of help vary widely. Providers and agencies at the local level should come together to understand one another's mandates and limitations. These conversations can serve as a springboard to creating effective local methods for responding to cases of financial exploitation in residential care.

Find out whether there is a local elder justice coalition, task force or coordinated response group working on abuse, neglect, and exploitation issues. If not, consider working with others to assemble a summit meeting to build cooperative approaches to financial exploitation cases. Joint training events are another effective approach to create and spread promising practices and to dispel myths about state laws and agency mandates.

Fraud and scams that target older people

Mrs. N began receiving sweepstakes offers in the mail shortly after her husband entered the nursing home. "They'd tell me I won and that all I had to do was send in $50 and I'd get free prizes, so I kept playing," she said. "They'd call me, too, and they were very nice on the phone." Pretty soon, Mrs. N was getting two or three calls a day and a grocery sack full of mail each week—news of "prizes" she had "won," but could collect only by sending anywhere from $50 to $2,000 by overnight mail. One day she asked a bank employee how she could send a large amount of cash through the mail. When the clerk heard what it was for, she examined Mrs. N's account transactions and found the elderly woman was writing as many as 90 checks a month to participate in sweepstakes games offering "free prizes."

Scams and fraud by strangers arise even in protected settings like assisted living and nursing facilities. Predators with a convincing story are as close as the telephone and the mailbox. For residents who use a computer to remain connected with family and friends, the computer can also be a source of scams.

Scams are always changing. This year's romance scam or grandparent fraud will be replaced by a new and creative scheme next year. The table on page 33 describes consumer scams that are common now, but keep your eyes open for new ones. The Federal Trade Commission has a "scam alert" page with information about the ever-changing ways that scam artists target consumers, at www.consumer.ftc.gov/scam-alerts.

Residents of assisted living and nursing facilities may be targets of predators who take advantage of victims' memory loss or their fear of a failing memory. For example, scammers may claim to be following up on a bogus order with a "payment" due. This is a double whammy. The victim is demeaned for "forgetting" and then robbed.

Here are some warning signs that scammers are victimizing a resident.

- The resident receives news about a prize or other windfall that requires payment of fees or taxes up front.

- The resident is pressured to keep good news a secret until a transaction is complete or risk losing out on this one-time opportunity.

- A caller constantly seeks more information and pressures the resident to comply.

- A third party claims to be from a government agency, financial institution or other entity and asks for information that they should already have.

- A resident receives a lot of mail or email for sweepstakes, contests or other sources suggesting that he or she has already been scammed.

Preventing predatory crimes requires our best efforts to raise awareness and ensure prompt response. To avoid identity theft, add safety features, such as antivirus software and password protection, to all facility-owned computers that are available to residents for personal use. Don't confiscate mail or monitor phone calls—those activities violate residents' rights. Use other strategies. Distribute alerts, bulletins, pamphlets and other resources to warn seniors and their families about scams, especially those that are prevalent nearby. These resources may be available from your state Attorney General's office, senior centers, ombudsman programs, national organizations and federal agencies. Conduct in-person programs for residents and families, such as *Money Smart for Older Adults* (see page 24).

If you believe that specific residents are the target of a telephone, mail, or computer scam, consider talking with their families or surrogates about your concern so that they can provide support and help to the resident in sorting the mail and discarding deceptive "offers."

Common Consumer Scams

Relative in need	Someone who pretends to be a family member or friend calls or e-mails you to say they are in trouble and need you to wire money right away.
Charity appeals	You get a call or letter from someone asking for money for a fake charity—either the charity does not exist or the charity did not call or write to you.
Lottery or sweepstakes	You get a call or e-mail that you have a chance to win a lot of money through a foreign country's sweepstakes or lottery. The caller will offer tips about how to win if you pay a fee or buy something. Or the caller or e-mail says you already have won and you must give your bank account information or pay a fee to collect your winnings.
Home improvement	Scammers take money for repairs and then they never return to do the work or they do bad work. Sometimes they break something to create more work or they say that things need work when they don't.
Free lunch	Scammers invite you to a free lunch and seminar, and then pressure you to give them information about your money, and to invest the money with them. They offer you "tips" or "guaranteed returns."
Free trip	Scammers say you've won a free trip but they ask for a credit card number or advance cash to hold the reservation.
Government money	You get a call or letter that seems to be from a government agency. Scammers say that if you give a credit card number or send a money order, you can apply for government help with housing, home repairs, utilities, or taxes.
Drug plans	Scammers pretend they are with Medicare prescription drug plans, and try to sell Medicare discount drug cards that are not valid. Companies with Medicare drug plans are not allowed to send unsolicited mail, emails, or phone calls.
Identity theft	Scammers steal personal information—such as a name, date of birth, Social Security number, account number, and mother's maiden name—and use the information to open credit cards or get a mortgage in someone else's name.
Fake "official" mail	Scammers send letters or e-mails that look like they are from a legitimate bank, business, or agency to try to get your personal information or bank account number.

Review

Together, we can work to combat financial exploitation of vulnerable adults, wherever they live. Here are the keys to success in congregate facilities.

- Understand what elder financial abuse is and the warning signs.

- Provide practical information to staff, residents, their families and others involved in their care about prevention and response to suspected exploitation.

- Respond quickly to delinquent accounts—i.e. 60 days/two billing cycles—and to unauthorized use of funds intended for the benefit of the resident (such as personal needs allowance accounts).

- Establish and maintain a well-coordinated team approach to financial security.

- Become skilled at recording and organizing information about suspected exploitation.

- Understand the responsibilities of mandated reporters, how to make a report, and how to follow up on reports.

- Learn to spot scams that can target any vulnerable people, especially those in care facilities.

- Know the roles of the long-term care ombudsmen, legal services programs and other service providers in your area.

- Have resources and contact numbers close at hand—and use them to prevent, recognize, record and report.

Resources for facilities, residents and families

In your community and state

Adult Protective Services
Find the state or local agencies that receive and investigate reports of suspected elder or adult abuse, neglect, or exploitation by contacting the national Eldercare Locator.

1-800-677-1116
www.eldercare.gov

Area Agency on Aging/Aging and Disability Resource Center
Find the local agencies that can give you information about aging and disability services—including local legal services programs and resources for caregivers—through the national Eldercare Locator.

1-800-677-1116
www.eldercare.gov

District attorney or prosecutor
Find your district attorney, city attorney or other prosecutor through the resources on the federal government's web portal.

www.answers.usa.gov/system/templates/selfservice/USAGov/#!portal/1012/article/3232/Locating-a-State-District-Attorney

Police or Sheriff
Find a law enforcement agency by checking the local directory.

Attorney General
Find a listing of state attorneys general on the website of the National Association of Attorneys General. Attorneys general can take action against consumer fraud.

www.naag.org

Elder care mediation
Mediation can help resolve disputes about caregiving and finances. Local attorneys, mental health professionals and mediation organizations may be able to provide listings of local mediators.

Long-term Care Ombudsman Program
The National Long-term Care Ombudsman Resource Center has detailed information on its website about ombudsman roles and programs at www.ltcombudsman.org. Find state and local long-term care ombudsman programs by contacting the national Eldercare Locator.

1-800-677-1116
www.eldercare.gov

Legal services

Free legal services for people over age 60
Find local programs that provide free legal help to people over age 60 by contacting the national Eldercare Locator.

1-800-677-1116
www.eldercare.gov

Free legal services for low-income people
Find local programs that provide free legal help to low-income people on the website of the Legal Services Corporation.

www.lsc.gov/find-legal-aid

Fee-for-service lawyers
A web page sponsored by the American Bar Association provides information about how to find a lawyer in each state.

www.findlegalhelp.org

Information on legal issues affecting residents
The National Legal Resource Center has information on financial security, guardianship, capacity and related topics.

www.nlrc.aoa.gov

Benefits

Benefits Check-up
BenefitsCheckUp, a free service of the National Council on Aging, helps adults age 55 and over identify benefits that could save them money and cover the costs of everyday expenses.

www.benefitscheckup.org

Medicaid/Medical Assistance
Find a listing of state agencies that provide Medicaid/Medical Assistance on the federal Benefits.gov website.

www.benefits.gov/benefits/browse-by-category/category/MED

Social Security
Find information about Social Security benefits, appeals, and representative payees.

www.socialsecurity.gov

Veterans Benefits
The Department of Veterans Affairs provides information about eligibility, health and long-term care benefits, and in-home care.

www.benefits.va.gov/benefits/

www.va.gov/opa/publications/benefits_book.asp

Resources for protecting residents against scams

Do Not Call Registry
The National Do Not Call Registry gives people a choice about whether to receive telemarketing calls (although scam artists may ignore the rules).

1-888-382-1222
www.donotcall.gov

Resources for health care professionals at your facility
The North American Securities Administrators Association provides links to information and resources to help identify elder fraud and financial exploitation—including a screening tool for clinicians.

www.nasaa.org/1733/eiffe/

Consumer Financial Protection Bureau
The CFPB takes complaints about consumer financial products and services, including credit cards, bank accounts and services, credit reporting and debt collection.

1-855-411-2372
www.consumerfinance.gov/complaint/

Stolen Social Security numbers
Report them to the Social Security Administration Fraud Hotline.

1-800-269-0271

Identifying and responding to scams
The Federal Trade Commission (FTC) website is a plentiful source of information for identifying and responding to scams, including those that target older people.

www.consumer.ftc.gov

Internet crimes
The FBI's Internet Crime Complaint Center has a two-page tip sheet on international internet scams at www.ic3.gov/media/MassMarketFraud.pdf and accepts complaints about internet crime.

www.ic3.gov

Scams by mail
Contact the United States Postal Inspection Service about any scams that use the US mail service.

1-877-876-2455
https://postalinspectors.uspis.gov/contactUs/filecomplaint.aspx

Terminology and usage in this manual

In this manual, we use the words and phrases defined below. Your state's terminology may differ regarding long-term services and supports, definitions of financial exploitation, and adult protective services (APS).

Adult protective services—social services programs provided by states nationwide, serving seniors and adults with disabilities who are in need of assistance. APS workers frequently serve as first responders in cases of abuse, neglect or exploitation. The National Adult Protective Services Association website provides information about how to report suspected abuse in each state. www.napsa-now. org/get-help/help-in-your-area.

Assisted living—residential care offering 24-hour staffing and assistance with activities of daily living. Assisted living is regulated by states. Over two-thirds of the states use the licensure term "assisted living" or a very similar term.

Elder abuse, often referred to as "abuse, neglect and exploitation," includes many types of mistreatment of older adults. The National Center on Elder Abuse describes seven types of elder abuse:

- Physical Abuse

- Sexual Abuse

- Emotional or Psychological Abuse

- Neglect

- Abandonment

- Financial or Material Exploitation

- Self-neglect.

Terminology for these types of elder abuse varies in state law.

Long-term Care Ombudsmen—advocates for residents of nursing homes, board and care homes, assisted living facilities and similar adult care facilities, in programs administered by the federal Administration on Aging/Administration for Community Living. Ombudsman staff and volunteers work to resolve problems of individual residents. Every state has an Office of the State Long-Term Care Ombudsman, headed by a full-time state ombudsman.

Mandatory reporters are people required by law required to report their suspicions about elder abuse to a specified public authority.

Mistreatment—abuse, neglect or exploitation, singly or in combination

Nursing facility—residential care facility subject to state licensure requirements as a "nursing home," "nursing facility," or "intermediate care facility," or providing similar levels of care. Most are also subject to federal standards as providers of Medicaid and/or Medicare covered services. Nursing facilities generally offer a higher level of care than assisted living facilities.

Vulnerable adult, person, or resident—an individual who is at risk of abuse, neglect or exploitation because of age or disability.

Endnotes

1   Manuals with state-specific information should not be designed in a manner that gives the impression that the guide is a CFPB product or has been officially endorsed by the Bureau. The CFPB logo should not be used, nor should the guide include any language to the effect that CFPB produced the material, endorses the final product, or has approved of it. States may indicate that their guide was based on a separate guide produced and distributed by CFPB.

2   This guide uses the terms "financial exploitation" and "financial abuse" interchangeably. Your state's laws that protect older adults may use these or other terms.

3   A few states have two separate agencies, one for people over age 60 or 65 and another for people from age 18 to age 60 or 65.

4   In addition to adult protective services laws, there may be other state or federal laws that require you and your staff to report suspected abuse or suspected crimes.

5   42 U.S.C. 1320b-25

6   The term "long-term care facility" means a residential care provider that arranges for, or directly provides, long-term care. The term "long-term care" means supportive and health services specified by the Secretary of the Department of Health and Human Services for individuals who need assistance because the individuals have a loss of capacity for self-care due to illness, disability, or vulnerability. 42 U.S.C. 1397j.

7   www.cms.gov/Medicare/Provider-Enrollment-and-Certification/ SurveyCertificationGenInfo/downloads/SCLetter11_30.pdf

8   For example, see www.fms.treas.gov/godirect/partners/nursing-facilities/. This link includes a federal government webinar that was developed in conjunction with the American Health Care Association.